D0382362

CHIPMUNK PORTRAIT

by

B. A. and H. K. HENISCH

with drawings by

H. S. WILSHER

THE CARNATION PRESS
State College, Pennsylvania
1970

UNIVERSITY OF VICTORIA
LIBRARY
Victoria, B. C.

ACKNOWLEDGEMENTS

We should like to thank the following, whose generous help made this book possible: Mrs. Elizabeth K. Henning of the Pattee Library, the Pennsylvania State University, University Park, Pennsylvania; Mrs. Marjorie Lambert of the Museum of New Mexico, Santa Fe, New Mexico; Mrs. Betty Toulouse of the Indian Arts Fund, Santa Fe, New Mexico; Mrs. Eleanor Pratt of the Museum of Anthropology, University of New Mexico, Albuquerque, New Mexico; Dr. and Mrs. Richard W. Lang, Mrs. Nedra Cook and Mr. Harry Walters of the Museum of Navaho Ceremonial Art, Santa Fe, New Mexico; and the Librarian and Staff of the General Library, British Museum (Natural History), London.

We are also grateful to Mr. Max Golding for two inspired guesses, to Miss Rebecca Cross for drawing our attention to the Beatrix Potter material and to Mrs. Sandra McBride for her forbearance and matchless skill in the preparation of the manuscript.

Special thanks are due to Chippy and her family, who posed with exemplary patience for all the nature photographs in this book.

B.A.H.

H.K.H.

Standard Book Number: 87601-003-6
Library of Congress Card No.: 78-88029

Copyright © 1970 by

THE CARNATION PRESS
P.O. Box 101
State College, Pennsylvania

Printed in the United States of America

To P. and R.

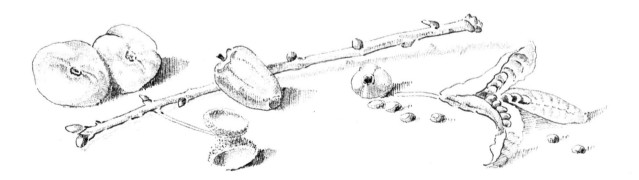

' It is a pleasing, pretty little domestic, and its tricks and habitudes may serve to entertain a mind unequal to stronger operations.' Oliver Goldsmith on the squirrel family, in his *History of the Earth and Animated Nature* (London, 1774).

The chipmunk is a small and lively member of the squirrel family. He climbs well but spends most of his time on the ground, where he makes his burrow. His call is sometimes a single sharp ' chip ', sometimes a loud steady repetition of the same note. With his passion for collecting, he is easily spotted in the right districts, bustling through woods and suburban gardens, cheek pouches crammed with supplies, intent on stocking yet another larder shelf. A lover of daylight, he is rarely seen out after dusk, and when winter weather becomes uncongenial he retires underground for a month or two. The color of his fur may vary from pale yellow to bright chestnut, but he is always strikingly marked on cheeks, back and sides with bold stripes in black and white. Though not actually domestic, he is certainly pleasing and pretty, with ' tricks and habitudes ' more entertaining to alerted minds than Goldsmith was prepared to allow. But then, Goldsmith had never seen a chipmunk; he knew him only from the scant reports available in his day.

For all his charm, circumstances have cheated the chipmunk of many compliments, because he chooses to make his home in regions which, until quite recently in history, were unknown or inaccessible to the inquiring traveller from Europe: parts of northern Russia, Siberia, Mongolia, northern China, Korea, northern Japan, and North America. Now that chipmunk watching is no longer the preserve of the daring and intrepid, an attempt at redress is long overdue. This book is concerned mostly with the chipmunk which lives in north-east America, but is offered as an affectionate tribute to chipmunks everywhere.

The discovery of such a small animal in a country as vast as America was of necessity a hit or miss affair, with luck and accident playing a decisive part. John Lawson, one of the first to discuss the chipmunk in any detail, owed his many years in the Carolinas to a chance conversation in London:

> ' In the year 1700 . . . my Intention, at that Time, being to travel, I accidentally met with a Gentleman, who had been Abroad . . . He assur'd me, that *Carolina* was the best Country I could go to; and that, there then lay a ship in the *Thames*, in which I might have my Passage. I laid hold on this Opportunity.' (1)

Later, while offering his own descriptive masterpiece to the Lords Proprietors of Carolina, he pointed out with the merest trace of complacency that many earlier travellers to America had been ill-equipped to give any clear picture of what they found there:

> ' 'Tis a great Misfortune, that most of our Travellers, who go to this vast Continent in America, are Persons of the meaner Sort, and generally of a very slender Education . . . incapable of giving any reasonable Account of what they met withal in those remote Parts; tho' the Country abounds with Curiosities worthy a nice Observation.' (2)

Lawson expected little else from the lower orders, but sometimes even their betters cravenly refused to try. Patrick M'Robert, another gentleman traveller from Britain, shrugged off the challenge:

> ' Were I an able naturalist, I might have given you a description of the different species of animals etc. to be found in this large country; but . . . I shall not attempt it.' (3)

In a less diffident mood, he might have spared a sentence for the chipmunk. Instead, we owe to him an elaborate table of stage fares between New York and Philadelphia.

Neither education nor curiosity were helpful to early travellers who had simply come to the wrong part of the country. The first English settlers in the 1580's touched only the coastline of Florida and Virginia where no chipmunk was to be found, and so none could be included in the terse list 'Of Beastes' drawn up by Thomas Hariot. More regrettably, none could figure in John White's lovely watercolors.

Gradually, however, reports trickled back to Europe from visitors delighted to play Adam in a new world and name the animals they had just discovered there. Gabriel Sagard, a French missionary, lived among the Indians in Canada from 1623 to 1624. Chipmunks crossed his path and must have lingered there on more than one occasion; "they bite like the damned" he notes with feeling and professional interest. Pain did not prevent him from coining an intriguing nickname for them: 'les Suisses' (4). Their markings may have reminded him of the striped, slashed uniform worn by the Swiss guards who had been in the service of the king of France since 1496. Perhaps somewhere at the back of his mind hovered also the phrase 'faire suisse', which means 'to eat or drink alone, without inviting one's friends'. Chipmunks, alas, were never genial hosts.

From 1663 to 1671 an Englishman, John Josselyn, was a guest at his brother's estate at Black Point, Massachusetts. He called his chipmunk Mouse Squirrel, and found its habits trying:

> 'The mouse squirril is hardly so big as a Rat, streak'd on both sides with black and red streaks. They are mischievous vermine destroying abundance of Corn both in the field and in the house, where they will gnaw holes into Chests, and tear clothes both linnen and wollen.' (5)

The name failed to stick. Clinging to the conviction that chipmunks dislike trees, most English visitors favored Ground Squirrel, a confusing choice today as it is now given to another member of the family, living in western America. Early in the eighteenth century John Lawson used the term in an affectionate if inaccurate paragraph:

> 'Ground Squirrels are so call'd, because they never delight in running up Trees, and leaping from Tree to Tree. They are the smallest of all Squirrels. Their Tail is neither so long nor bushy; but flattish. They are of a reddish Colour, and striped down each Side with black Rows, which make them very beautiful.

They may be kept tame, in a little Box
with Cotton. They and the Flying
Squirrels seldom stir out in Cold
Weather, being tender Animals.' (6)

Peter Kalm, a Swedish scientist, pupil and
colleague of Linné, or Linnaeus, was sent on
an expedition to America between 1748 and
1751. Travelling through Pennsylvania, he
made this entry in his journal on November
14th, 1748:

'There is small species of squirrels
abounding in the woods, which the
English call ground squirrels . . . Dr.
Linné calls it *Sciurus striatus*, or the
streaked squirrel.' (7)

Such observers and their counterparts in
other countries made their notes on the spot.
At home in Europe the synthesizing naturalists, Ray, Buffon, Pennant, sat in their studies,
waiting like spiders for letters to fly into the
web. With patient ingenuity each stitched the
jumble of reports from far-flung correspondents into his own elaborate patchwork, an
Histoire naturelle here, a *Synopsis of Quadrupeds*
there. Explorers in the field were not always
gratified by the finished product, especially

when they found their own contribution distorted, ignored or used without acknowledgement. In the hope of improving a second edition, Peter Pallas, who travelled in Russia, sent off to Thomas Pennant (1726–98) a long list of the mistakes and misunderstandings he had discovered in the latter's book, with a note at once disarming and diplomatic:

> ' I know your love of truth is such, that you will not take amiss my mentioning to you, what chance gave me an opportunity of observing more accurately.' (8)

Despite all drawbacks, current practice made it possible for John Ray, in England, to gather enough material for a comparison between Russian and American chipmunks. In his *Synopsis Methodica Animalium* (London, 1693), he found them very much alike.

In the eighteenth century, the name by which the chipmunk was known varied widely, depending as it did on whatever sources an author could lay his hands on when composing his *Chapter on the Squirrel Family*. John Lawson and Mark Catesby had spotted the chipmunk in Carolina, and so, for their followers like Oliver Goldsmith, he became ' the little ground squirrel of Carolina ' (9). William Bartram, the Philadelphia naturalist, had lots of chipmunks in his own garden, but found none in his travels to ' the maritime parts of Carolina

and the Floridas '. For him and his supporters the chipmunk was 'the little striped squirrel of Pennsylvania' (10). The Comte de Buffon used one of Peter Kalm's terms, ' the little ground squirrel' and, like him, placed it in Pennsylvania, but also referred to ' the striped squirrel of Canada', perhaps remembering Sagard (11).

Whatever the qualifying adjective, ground, striped, Carolina, Canadian, Pennsylvania, even mouse, the chipmunk remained for most naturalists a squirrel. Thomas Pennant struck out on a line of his own. Noting the animal's habit of sleeping through the winter, he called it the Striped Dormouse, and classified it accordingly (12). When Thomas Bewick, the Newcastle wood engraver, came to picture the chipmunk in his *History of Quadrupeds* (1785–90), he cautiously covered all options by labelling his illustration ' The Dormouse or Ground Squirrel'.

It was early in the nineteenth century that the chipmunk of north-east America was settled at last in the official niche it occupies today. In 1811 Illiger declared it to be a member of the squirrel family, but within that large group placed it in a class by itself with its own generic name: *tamias striatus*. This, inspired not by the chipmunk's winter habits but by its passion for possessions, may be translated as Striped Steward. Stewards organize and arrange their master's belongings and stock his larders; they have therefore something in common with chipmunks, though it is doubtful whether the latter would find real satisfaction in diligent housekeeping for somebody else. The same reservation would be shared, no doubt, by all chipmunks. Yet, with a touch of partiality, the name *eutamias*, Good Steward, has been awarded to the chipmunks, smaller and with a slightly different tooth structure, which live in western America, Russia and Asia (13).

While accepted as one of the squirrel family, the *Sciuridae*, the chipmunk is usually regarded as a junior member. A nineteenth century Canadian writer, Mrs. Catherine Traill, in her story *The History of a Squirrel Family*, pictures him as a poor relation bullied by his large and bouncing cousins (14). The fossil evidence, gratifyingly, tells another tale. It suggests a role for the chipmunk much closer to that of founder-member of the entire tribe, and places him, not on some insignificant twig but on the main stem of the family tree. Its branches are occupied by many different animals: squirrels, flying squirrels, ground squirrels, marmots, woodchucks, prairie dogs. Some, like the squirrels, live mainly in trees; others, like the woodchucks, mainly on the ground. The chipmunk is at ease in both. His remains appear early in the fossil record,

distinguishable as a separate stock at least since the late Oligocene period. Craig C. Black, in his *Review of the North American Tertiary Sciuridae* says:

> ' Recent chipmunks, in both their morphology and ecology, stand in an intermediate position between the tree squirrels and the ground squirrels. They are capable climbers, and will cache food in trees, but are for the most part terrestrial, living in burrows and foraging on the ground. They inhabit forest to forest edge environments and are nut, seed, and berry eaters. I visualize the ancestral squirrels as being chipmunk-like. Such animals would be well suited to make the shift into an open grassland habitat as well as being adapted for an arboreal habit.' (15)

Tamias is thought to have lived only in North America, but early fossil remains of *eutamias* have been found in northwest America and northeast Asia. It is assumed that he made the journey across the Bering Strait when it was a land bridge, but where his stock began and how he travelled, from east to west or from west to east, remain problems tantalizingly unsolved.

Living in happy obscurity, the chipmunk was destined to receive few tributes from writers and artists, even after the discovery of the New World. More exotic creatures, the opossums, the hummingbirds and the crab-catching raccoons caught the fancy of Europe, while one spectacular cousin, the flying squirrel, stole his thunder. As early as 1610 the Earl of Southampton rashly described this creature to James I and found himself forthwith commissioned to obtain one. His letter of enquiry to a friend ends on a weary note:

> 'I would not have troubled you with
> this but that you know so well how
> he is affected to these toys.' (16)

Neither flying squirrel nor chipmunk could share the collation of best bread and butter spread each morning by Horace Walpole for the elegant squirrels of Strawberry Hill. Coleridge mined Bartram's journal for exotic details, but since chipmunks had failed to find a place there, none could appear in his poems. Bartram's crocodiles, by their very nature more likely to bring an acquisitive gleam to a Romantic's eye, managed to squeeze in (17).

Inevitably, the chipmunk peeps for a moment from the pages of nineteenth century American books. Thoreau caught a glimpse of him one Tuesday morning on the bank of a river:

> 'The chipping or striped squirrel sat
> upon the end of some Virginia fence
> . . . twirling a green nut with one paw,
> as in a lathe, while the other held it
> fast against its incisors as chisels.' (18)

Only in 1911 did he slip into a starring role and the mainstream of European literature, when Beatrix Potter placed him disconcertingly within her very English countryside in *The Tale of Timmy Tiptoes*. Why she chose to do so remains a puzzle, and students of her work can merely hint at answers. Certainly she was, as she once bluffly remarked, extremely fond of all 'little rubbish': mice, guinea-pigs, squirrels. One of her many young correspondents in America may have asked her for a story about chipmunks. With her known interest in American books for children, it is possible that she found suggestions for her plot in Catherine Traill's account of squirrel adventures, reprinted time and again between 1850 and 1900. Once intrigued by the subject she could have made her own observations and sketches at the London Zoo, where chipmunks were alive and well continuously between 1880 and 1911 (19).

Anana   *Cornus*

It was late for an animal to make its debut. Accidents of geography forbade the chipmunk's introduction to the manuscript illuminators of medieval Europe. But for these, he would have taken his place to the manner born in their pages, climbing the tendrils of an intricate border, sheltering in the curve of an acanthus leaf, placidly munching a strawberry while offering his back as footstool or lectern to some excited prophet.

In the end, not artists but early naturalists provided the first formal portraits. One of the best appears in Mark Catesby's *Natural History of Carolina, Florida and the Bahama Islands* (London, 1731–43). According to Peter Kalm, this was drawn by Catesby from life; certainly it has a vitality, not to mention verisimilitude, noticeably lacking in some of the others. Another was drawn by George Edwards a few years later, for his *Natural History of Birds* (London, 1743–51). Edwards himself never visited America, but his helpful note explains where he studied his model and provides a gentle puff for his own book, with a dig at Catesby's:

From Mark Catesby's *Natural History* (1731–43). University of Pennsylvania Library.

'This Squirrel was the Property of Sir *Hans Sloane*, Bart. They are brought from *Carolina*, and other parts of *North-America*. It has been figur'd and describ'd by my late Friend, Mr. *Catesby*, in his *History of Carolina, Vol.* II. P. 75, but as that expensive Work will fall into but few Hands, I hope this Figure will prove acceptable to most of my Encouragers.' (20)

The chipmunk he sketched was probably not alive but preserved. *The Gentleman's Magazine* for July, 1748, describes a visit by the Prince and Princess of Wales to the house of Sir Hans Sloane in Chelsea, where they found 'the great saloon lined on every side with bottles filled with spirits, containing various animals.' Sloane, whose vast collection was to form the nucleus of the British Museum after his death, knew from bitter experience the agony of attempting to bring a live specimen home from abroad. In his early days he made a voyage to the West Indies and was delighted to find in Jamaica an amiable seven-foot snake which used to follow its master like a dog. Sloane tried to keep it alive for the homeward journey in a water jar, but one day it escaped and ventured into the servants' living quarters. There, after several days, an intolerant footman killed it, much to the puzzlement of Sir Hans, who had thought the snake admirably accommodated:

From George Edwards' *Natural History of Birds* (1743–51). Pennsylvania State Library.

'It seemed, before this disaster, to be very well pleased with its situation, being in a part of the house which was filled with rats, which are the most pleasing food for these sort of serpents.' (21)

It may be assumed with confidence that any specimen approved by Sloane was preserved with all the skill available at the time. An artist without access to such a museum and without chance to see a live model was in real difficulty. He could copy an existing engraving, in good faith but without means of checking its accuracy. In his *Memoir*, Thomas Bewick explained:

> ' Such animals as I knew, I drew from memory on the wood; others which I did not know were copied from " Dr. Smellie's Abridgement of Buffon ", and other naturalists, and also from the animals which were from time to time exhibited in itinerant collections.' (22)

The chipmunk in Smellie's book was engraved by his friend, Andrew Bell, incidentally the first proprietor of the Encyclopaedia Britannica (1771), but no better acquainted with the animal than Bewick himself. Alternatively, he could work from some skin or stuffed specimen which had found its way to Europe. Thomas Pennant mentions in an aside that chipmunk skins " are of little use but are sometimes brought over to line cloaks." Many samples must have arrived in a pitiably bedraggled condition, pickled inexpertly in rum or packed for months in tar-sealed chests which would not have satisfied Sir Hans. Some were badly moth-eaten, a

Engraving by Andrew Bell, for Smellie's *Abridgement of Buffon's Natural History* (1781). By permission of the Trustees of the British Museum (Natural History).

Below:
woodcut by Thomas Bewick, from his *History of Quadrupeds* (1785–90).

Above: from John Brickell's *Natural History of North Carolina* (1737). By permission of the Trustees of the British Museum (Natural History).

Below: from Peter Kalm's *Travels in North America* (English edition of 1770).

condition not merely unattractive but positively misleading. Samuel Dale, writing to Sloane, pointed out the error of the great seventeenth-century naturalist, John Ray, who had placed the flying squirrel in the mouse family because the tail of his specimen happened to be hairless, not bushy like that of proper squirrels:

> ' Which Mistake may perhaps arise from only seeing the Skin of one dead, when the Hair of the Tail had been eaten off by *Mites*, for in one that I did see alive, which was brought over from *Virginia* by Madam Cock, Sister to Mr. *Catesby*, the Tail was hairy, as in others of the *Squirrel-kind*.' (23)

The gloomy and lethargic chipmunk which crept into the 1770 English translation of Peter Kalm's *Travels*, is by an unknown hand, guided by inadequate clues. The illustrator of John Brickell's *Natural History of North Carolina* (Dublin, 1737), obviously disdained the help of engraving, specimen or skin, as his chipmunk is covered in spots from head to toe. He even disdained the help of his own author, who refers explicitly to ground squirrels ' finely striped . . . like the young Fawns ' (24). Rumor may have helped to shape the artist's fancy. John Clayton, in a paper for the Royal Society in 1693, listed three kinds of squirrel in Virginia, and remarked:

'The Third is the Ground Squirrel. I never saw any of this sort, only I have been told of them, and have had them described to me, to be little bigger than a Mouse, finely spotted like a young Fawn.' (25)

Spotted or striped, that was the question. Brickell, an assiduous borrower from earlier naturalists, may have hit upon the truth by a carefree misreading of Clayton's words. The last in this group of early portraits is from Audubon's *Quadrupeds of North America* (1849–54) and demonstrates again the advantage of first-hand knowledge.

While long a stranger to Europe, the chipmunk had a firm place in the affections and heritage of the American Indian. It is widely assumed that his modern name was originally suggested by his unmistakable 'chip, chip' call. In fact it is an anglicized corruption of an Indian word for the red squirrel. This was written down by white settlers sometimes as *adjidaumo*, sometimes as *atchitamon*. When a vocabulary of Chippewa Indian words was drawn up by Long in 1791, he rendered their word for squirrel as *chetamon*, and it is from this that the modern *chipmunk* developed, by way of *chitmunk*. The Chippewa Indians lived in the Great Lakes region. In her book *The Canadian Crusoes* (1850), which is explicitly set in Chippewa country, Mrs. Traill writes: 'We hear the cry of squirrels and *chitmunks*.' Here,

From J. J. Audubon's *Quadrupeds of North America* (*1849-54*).

and in succeeding editions of her *Stories of the Canadian Forest*, right into the 1870's, the spelling *chitmunk* is always used. By 1895, however, in her *Cot and Cradle Stories* she had surrendered to the misconception still popular today: ' The Indians call the ground squirrels *chipmunks* because . . . they cry chip-chip-chip ' (26).

The word *adjidaumo* or *atchitamon* means
' head first ' and refers to the squirrel's charac-
teristic way of coming down trees. Longfellow's
translation in *Hiawatha* (1855) is a little
different. His hero, helped by a squirrel,
exclaims:

' Take the thanks of Hiawatha,
And the name which now he
    gives you,
For hereafter and forever
Boys shall call you *Adjidaumo*,
Tail-in-air the boys shall call you.'

Fractious precisionists, dismayed by the elusiveness of truth, must draw what comfort they can from the knowledge that either translation fits squirrels and chipmunks equally well.

'Chipmunk' was never used by the first European travellers and naturalists. Significantly, a version of it ('chipmuck') makes its appearance in James De Kay's *Zoology of New York* (Albany, New York, 1842–4), and the modern word itself in Audubon's *Quadrupeds of North America* (1849–54), both books written by men who had lived in America for many years and were completely familiar with the popular, local names of the animals they described. The victory of 'chipmunk' over its rivals was slow. In his journal of the 1850's, Thoreau uses a variety of terms, including chipmunk, ground squirrel and chip squirrel, but his favorite is striped squirrel. In one entry, for October 8th, 1857, he refers to 'the chipmunk, the wall-going squirrel', a name interestingly similar to the one used by the Pennsylvania Dutch: 'fensermaus' or fence-mouse.

In Indian legend the chipmunk plays a virtuous role, flawed only once in a Navaho story by a weakness for filching tobacco pouches. Even then there were extenuating circumstances, for Chipmunk stole in a time of famine, and the tobacco pouch he chose contained a little piece of fat. It belonged, moreover, to Coyote, a creature more than capable of looking after his own interests (27). This one lapse apart, Chipmunk is on the side of light against darkness, of right against wrong, with a kindly interest in human welfare. The Navaho taboo 'Never kill a chipmunk' rests on the belief that he will lead travellers to food and water. Navahos make prayer sticks to him, yellow, striped with black, topped with feathers, inset with shell, turquoise and jet. A certain plant which the Navahos call 'chipmunk food' is known to be an excellent protection against the unwanted attentions of hostile ghosts, who much dislike its smell. The lion may roar and the snake hiss; characteristically, Chipmunk makes his displeasure felt by giving his tormentors a tickle in the nose. When children scratch their noses, parents can be sure they have been teasing chipmunks. In Navaho myths about the creation, First Man, First Woman and certain privileged animals emerged into the world and helped each other. No distinction was made between them, and all are spoken of as 'First People'. Chipmunk is numbered among this honored company.

Being both inquisitive and inconspicuous, Chipmunk can keep an unobtrusive watch on the wicked. The most wicked, and certainly the wiliest of the Navaho animals is Coyote, quite as shameless and ingenious in his own way as Reynard the fox is in Europe. Coyote comes unscathed through innumerable adventures by the simple precaution of burying his vital parts, heart, lungs, breath and blood in a safe place before trotting off, smugly invulnerable. A caprice of uncharacteristic generosity leads him one day to share the secret of his success with a singularly disagreeable girl, herself a villain of the first water. While she is hiding her own innards she fails to notice Chipmunk, alert in the shadow of a bush. By chirping loudly, Chipmunk draws the girl's virtuous brother to the hiding place, where he proceeds to kill her *in absentia*.

Many tales link the chipmunk and the bear in uneasy partnership; in Russia, one of the pet names for a chipmunk is 'the bear's conscience' (28). The phrase suggests admirably their relationship in Indian folklore where the tiny and, truth to tell, insufferably righteous chipmunk goads the lumbering bear beyond endurance. One evening, the Iroquois say, the porcupine gathered all the animals together to debate whether to have perpetual night or perpetual day. The bear rumbled away, 'Night is best, we must have darkness', while the chipmunk needled him by chirping all night long, ' Light will come, we must have light '. The bear's simmering irritation boiled over when the sky began to lighten and the chipmunk's chant became a victory song. A great paw shot out and the tormentor bolted to safety, but not before his back was striped for ever by the claws (29).

The Thompson River Indians of British Columbia thought that the chipmunk's song sounded like the noise of a fire when fresh wood is thrown on. In their version, Bear and Chipmunk quarrel about a log burning on top of a mountain. Bear, hating light, tries to trample it out, while Chipmunk pirouettes between his legs, stoking it with twigs. Once again the paw shoots out, once again the victim escapes, once again his back is marked forever (30).

A more gracious story is told in India to explain the markings on the striped squirrel. He helped the god Rama to cross the sea between India and Ceylon, and to thank him Rama gently stroked his back, leaving the imprint of three fingers (31). For the Navahos, too, the chipmunk's stripes were given as a reward, not in revenge. When a hero had killed an alarming monster he prudently asked Chipmunk to run over the creature's horns and make quite certain it was really dead. Having accomplished his mission and sung out reassurance in his usual jaunty way, Chipmunk was invited to streak his face and body with the monster's blood.

One of Chipmunk's less successful diagnoses is recorded in another Navaho story. Guileful Coyote decided to make sure of a good dinner by lying flat on his back, pretending to be dead. One by one the little animals crept up, nosed him cautiously and scurried off to report their findings to anxious friends. Each thought Coyote had died, but none inspired confidence. At last, reliable Chipmunk was dispatched. He boldly leapt onto Coyote's stomach, pattered up and down and returned to announce authoritatively that the arch-enemy was no more. A celebration dance began round the body, only to be rudely interrupted when Coyote sprang to his feet and gobbled everybody up. Fortunately, mistakes in folklore are never final. Coyote may lick his lips in one round, but Chipmunk is sure to bounce back in the next with reputation unscathed.

Chipmunk's preference for life on the ground helped to shape a legend told by the Algonquin Indians of New England. Two sisters married stars, and for a long time lived happily up in the sky. One day they rashly lifted up a stone they had been forbidden to touch. Underneath was a hole, through which they could see, glimmering far below, the earth they had almost forgotten. Begged and badgered to let them go home, their husbands at last agreed and devised for them an ingenious re-entry program. The sisters were told to sleep together and not to open their eyes until they

Head mask. Photograph by courtesy of
the Museum of the American Indian.
Heye Foundation, New York.

had heard three songs: the chickadee's, the
red squirrel's and the chipmunk's. At first
obedient, the wives kept their eyes tightly
closed through the bird's song, but when the
squirrel began to chatter they could hold out
no longer. They peeped, and found themselves
perched on the top of a tall pine tree. Had
they waited a moment longer, they would have
landed gently in the grass, right beside the
chipmunk (32).

The Hopi Indians of the south-western
states worship kachinas, the spirits of natural
forces, plants, birds and animals which play a
significant part in Hopi life. At their festivals,
men in elaborate masks and costumes imper-
sonate the various kachinas. Small dolls,

Chipmunk kachina, sketched by Fewkes, in *The 21st Annual Report of the Bureau of American Ethnology to the Secretary of the Smithsonian Institution*, by J. W. Powell (1903).

dressed in the same way, are made for children, to help them learn to identify each kachina's distinctive attributes (33). The chipmunk is one of several Runner Kachinas which challenge Hopi men to race during the festivities. If the men win, the kachinas give them presents; if they lose, they are punished in some way. The chipmunk kachina beats his victim with a yucca leaf whip. A sketch, made in 1899 to illustrate an essay by Jesse Walter Fewkes, shows a chipmunk kachina with his head mask and body striped, and yucca whips in his hands. A modern full-length portrait was drawn in 1957 by a Hopi artist, Leroy Kewanyama, of Shungopawy, Arizona. A

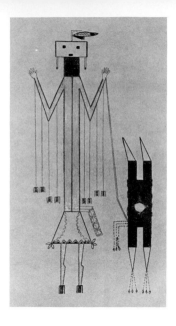

Navaho Plumeway sand painting, copied by Mrs. Rebecca Lang, Museum of Navaho Ceremonial Art, Santa Fe, New Mexico.

typical head mask is made of yellow rawhide, with stripes of white, black and red between the eyes and a collar of rags or fur. Kachina dolls in great variety are a popular tourist item in the south west, but the chipmunk form, of which an endearing example is here shown, is now a rarity.

Chipmunk also appears in a Navaho sandpainting, usually made on the second day of the Plumeway ceremony (34). This is a ritual performed to cure certain diseases of the head and eyes, and infection from game animals. Chipmunk and his wife have a place among

Chipmunk kachina, painted by Leroy Kewanyama, Shungopawy, Arizona. School of American Research, Santa Fe, New Mexico.

many creatures depicted in the Plumeway paintings, because their special plant, ' chipmunk food ', is used as a medicine during the proceedings. The figure illustrated here has a yellow body and a white, rectangular mask. This is normally the female mask, and is thought to represent Chipmunk's wife. She is known as the spirit of sunset, and on the tobacco pouch or medicine bag she carries is a white moon, edged with red sparrowhawk feathers. The pendants hanging from the pouch are fawn toes, delightfully called ' deer-toe twinklers '.

Hopi kachina doll,
from the collection of Mrs. Marjorie Lambert, Museum of
New Mexico, Santa Fe, New Mexico.

Hard on the heels of history and legend come the chipmunks of today, and among a host of contemporaries are the distinguished envoys accredited to the authors' garden. This patch of land basks in the brilliant sunshine of central Pennsylvania, but is shaded by several trees, yielding a welcome harvest of cherries and hazelnuts. A grape vine is trained behind two flower beds, which are terraced by low rock walls and divided from one another by a shallow flight of steps. This forms a natural boundary, carefully noted, if not always respected, by skirmishing chipmunks which compete for the whole coveted area. Beneath the flower beds the ground is honey-combed by tunnels, running back from innumerable nooks and crannies in the walls and emerging here and there under the vine. The walls make natural lookout posts, where guard duty may be pleasantly combined with preening and sunbathing. Small dishes of water have been set between the stones, and food is to be found with only a trifle more exertion at a bird feeder a little distance away.

The whole scene may be surveyed with ease
from a window under which is piled a heap of
logs, inspected regularly by birds and animals
for nuts, seeds, water and ants.

Several chipmunks pay visits and some take
out permanent squatters' rights, but the oldest
official resident has lived there for at least three
years. This is a female named, with some lack
of originality, Chippy. As all chipmunks seem
equally glossy, charming and elusive, practice
is needed before one can be distinguished from
another with any confidence. Conveniently
for amateur naturalists, chipmunks nip each
other when they fight, and the part of their
anatomy which comes most readily to mouth
is the tail. Chippy's was rudely shortened one
day to a pitiful, ragged stump, which time and
meticulous grooming has transformed into a
handsome lion's tail, still short but topped with
an impressive tuft of hair. Its shape, quite
unlike the long, straight line of the classic
chipmunk tail, separates Chippy from her
peers.

However, such battle scars are fashionable among chipmunks, and even the most eye-catching tail is not always displayed to the best advantage, but may be hidden inconsiderately from view. One of the surest ways to pick out a special chipmunk is to know his daily habits. Chipmunks are conservative. Three may visit a bird feeder at the same time, and each will leave by his own familiar route. In search of food they will pop in and out of a hundred holes in a rock wall, but each will hurry back to the one he regards as home. A clear passage to this front door is of the first importance. Once, while Chippy was away collecting a peanut, an enormous sunflower head, bursting with ripe seeds, was laid over her main entrance by a well-meaning but misguided donor. Finding this road-block on her return, she was too agitated to appreciate the unexpected treasure-trove. Not until the head had been shifted to clear the way did she show any interest in the feast to come. The need for clear access may be the reason why entrances are made at some distance from the principal food collection centers. Chippy finds provisions at certain places on the stone wall, and has to scramble for these supplies with highly interested competitors. Nevertheless she chooses to lose time carrying each precious load home to her quiet, unmolested entrance several yards away, safe from the jostling of blue jays and the unwelcome attentions of red squirrels.

Chipmunks hibernate in a football-shaped cavity a few feet underground, at any rate during the worst of winter, and the time when they emerge to start a new year varies widely. The Delaware Indians of south-east Pennsylvania and Maryland used to call January ' ground squirrel month ', the time when chipmunks come out of their holes (35). In 1968 Chippy herself was first seen on February 16th. In 1802, William Bartram, the Philadelphia naturalist, noted in his diary:

> ' February 17. The ground squirrel came out of his winter quarters, frisking about in the warm sun.' (36)

In 1969, on the other hand, while one male chipmunk was out in the garden by February 21st, Chippy herself was not seen until March 19th. In colder New York state, this is the month when chipmunks are first regularly seen (37).

The decision to brave the elements cannot depend entirely on temperature. Part of January is often mild in north-east America, while February and March may be bitter. First thoughts of mating probably have more influence than weather or dwindling food supplies. For a week or two the chipmunk is out only briefly each day; when a particularly wicked wind is curling round, Chippy waits prudently for the sun to reach the stone wall before hunching there in gloomy meditation for a few minutes. February and March are the best months of the year to see the chipmunk's clear, elegant tracks in light snow which does not hinder his activities. A heavy fall will keep him underground for a few days, but Chippy herself has been seen on occasion, shooting up like a small brown periscope from a smooth, unsullied wave of snow, to reconnoitre for a moment before sinking out of sight.

Mating takes place quite soon after the beginning of the chipmunk year; indeed some males are ready to mate in February. They must explore to find a female, while Chippy sits sedately in her kingdom, waiting for visitors. In 1968 one arrived on March 7th and the whole ceremonial took three days to complete. After this the male vanished as suddenly as he had appeared, in search, presumably, of fresh adventures. Certainly the resident male in the garden disappeared several times in the spring of 1969 for a period of two or three days. Thirty-one days pass before the babies are born, naked, blind and usually about four in number. They spend six weeks underground and at last climb out into the sunshine of mid-May, a little uncertain on their legs but otherwise confident, inquisitive and about three-quarters the size of their harassed mother. Delighted investigation of a new world follows for ten days or so. Vines and flowers in which Chippy herself has long lost interest are carefully inspected and, with just a touch of original

sin, occasionally eaten. In the end, maternal anxiety changes to irritation and Chippy begins to chase her offspring out of her territory. Several days of determined bullying are needed to convince the most obtuse baby that he is no longer a cosseted member of the family, merely an unwelcome guest. Then, one morning, the garden is at peace, and Chippy sits washing on the wall, luxuriating in solitude.

High summer, with its lazy warmth and food for the taking everywhere, is usually a drowsy time. Indeed, chipmunks can be so quiet in July and August that naturalists have sometimes thought they retire for a period of aestivation, summer's ' hibernation ' (38). Despite the insistence of Indian legends on chipmunks' love of light, they do not enjoy blazing sunshine and intense heat, showing far more energy on a cool, damp, grey morning than at burning noon. In the fierce dog days of summer they tend to make their appearance early in the morning or late in the afternoon when the sun's sting has been drawn. With underground burrows and well-stocked larders they can arrange their timetable to suit the day's condition and their own convenience. Such sensible independence makes them elusive at this period.

There is a second mating season round about July, after which males lose their interest in females until the next year. They become less quarrelsome and their new-found calm makes its own contribution to the sleepiness of summer. In one year Chippy's new family was scrambling over the stone wall by the first days of September; in another, though mating took place on July 10th, no babies were born.

The pace of life quickens again in early fall and there is a steady crescendo of excitement as everything edible is harvested for the long winter. Chipmunks bustle about, shining like chestnuts among the sweet rotting apples, the acorns and the crackling leaves. As John Josselyn remarked:

> ' When hasel and filbert nuts are ripe
> you may see upon every Nut-tree as
> many mouse-squirrels as leaves.' (39)

In his journal on October 27, 1857, Thoreau records the experience of a friend who happened to walk under an oak tree:

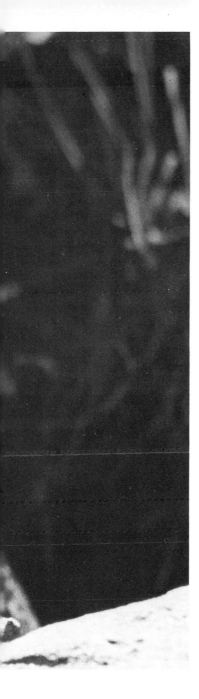

' The *dust* of acorn shells (or cups?)
was falling about him. Looking up
he saw as many as twenty (!) striped
squirrels busily . . . stowing the nuts
away in their cheeks.'

This is the time when chipmunks find their
way unerringly to bags of peanuts hidden deep
in locked garages. They empty bird feeders
with the efficiency of high-powered vacuum
cleaners, and do their best to support Cotgrave's double definition of an old French
word:

' *Escureur*; a Squirrell; also, a Scowrer,
cleanser.' (40)

Some hibernating animals, like the woodchuck, store their food by eating it, adding
layers of fat to sustain them through their deep
winter sleep. The chipmunk stays as slim as
ever, and concentrates on filling his capacious
larders to overflowing. Only when convinced
that he has enough to tide him over the winter
months does he relax. For the last week or
two before retirement there is a noticeable
slackening of interest in food. On two memor-
able occasions, Chippy herself was seen to pass
a peanut without a second glance.

The date when hibernation begins varies
as much as the date it ends. In 1967 Chippy
was out in a flurry of snow on Christmas Day,
while in 1968 she retired on November 4th (41).
A true hibernator, like the woodchuck, sinks

UNIVERSITY OF VICTORIA
LIBRARY
Victoria, B. C.

into a deep coma in which he remains throughout the winter. The chipmunk is sometimes in a torpor, sometimes merely dazed with sleep, sometimes alert and bursting with housewifely energy. Unlike the princess disconcerted by one pea beneath her twenty mattresses, the chipmunk can relax only when he knows his bed is made entirely of food. Nothing so reassures him as the comforting pressure of a thousand nuts and seeds, lightly blanketed by wisps of grass and withered leaves. Mounds of food are piled on every side, and in this edible cocoon winter passes as one long midnight snack, enjoyed in bed with eyes tight shut. The chipmunk has been heard singing softly to himself while fast asleep, occasionally jerking from some nightmare of under-nourishment with a sharp 'chip' of alarm (42).

Like the golden hamster, the chipmunk is clean and orderly; it is at some distance from his bed that he makes his midden heap, to which he proceeds with a sleep-walker's dignity. Eating in bed has many charms but one drawback: steadily accumulating debris. A plump sunflower seed delights the chipmunk senses; an empty husk is but a hollow mockery. Chipmunks cope with the problem by waking up sufficiently often to open new passageways and tidy their rubbish away in old ones. When Chippy herself emerges each spring she uses a front door quite different from that favored the previous autumn.

All the year round chipmunks like to dig almost as much as they love to collect food. For an animal whose main defence against attack is the ability to make a lightning getaway, tunnels winding safely home are a necessity. In the course of time, prudence and self-indulgence combine to create an intricate subterranean maze which also provides a varied playground for the babies.

So much digging creates large quantities of unwanted soil which are removed in several ways. Naturalists have observed the chipmunk at times pushing soil out of a hole with his nose, at times carrying it away in his pouches. In the first case the fresh earth is very finely crumbled, in the second it is in the form of larger pellets (43). One male in the garden has been seen shovelling with furious energy, using his forelegs like a dog to send the earth flying behind him. Whatever the favored style, the little tell-tale heaps are never allowed to draw attention by their presence to the front door itself.

The basic necessities of a burrow are quite simple. The main entrance tunnel runs down

gradually to a depth of two or three feet, just below the frost line, and there widens into the nesting chamber. This is large, about one foot in diameter, in order to accommodate the bed of food. A little to one side is the midden heap and running off are tunnels for storage and for rubbish. Some observers, both in Russia and America, have reported that the chipmunk keeps different foods in separate larders. Here is Peter Kalm's account:

'When a Swede once pretty late in autumn was digging for a mill dam in a neighboring hill, he came upon a subterranean passage belonging to these squirrels (chipmunks). He followed it for some time, and discovered a walk on one side like a branch from the chief stem. It was nearly two feet long, and at its end had a quantity of choice acorns of the white oak, which the little foresighted animal had stored up for the winter. Soon after he found another passage on the side like the former, but containing a fine store of corn; the next had hickory nuts; and the last and most hidden one contained some excellent chestnuts, to an amount which might have filled two hats.' (44)

However stored, the amount of food collected is large: more than half a bushel of hickory nuts and acorns has been found in one burrow; four quarts of seeds, including 250,000 wild buckwheat seeds, in another (45). Chipmunks are reputed to have a stern eye for quality as well as quantity. In Russia ' chipmunk nuts ' fetch higher prices in the market than those gathered by men, for while to err is human, chipmunks never give house-room to a second-rate nut (46). Thoreau noted in his journal on August 29th, 1858, that the hazelnut harvest had been carried off by chipmunks:

> ' Every nut that I could find left in
> that field was a poor one.'

Early naturalists noted other evidence of chipmunk concern for quality control. Thomas Pennant, quietly borrowing from Peter Kalm, remarked of his ' striped dormouse ':

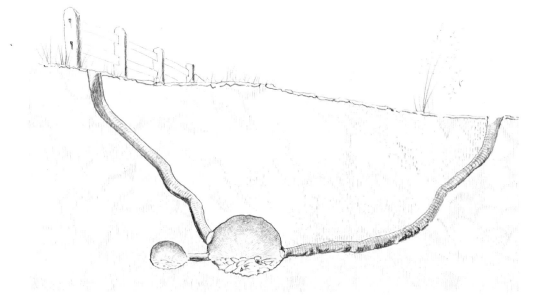

' It is observable that they give great preference to certain food; for if, after filling their mouths with rye, they happen to meet with wheat, they fling away the first, that they may indulge in the last.' (47)

Contemporary chipmunks have less discriminating palates than their eighteenth-century ancestors. When examining a heap of nuts and seeds Chippy may pick and choose, sometimes concentrating on sunflower seeds, sometimes on peanuts, but never has she been seen to discard anything edible. Her taste in food is eclectic. No nut comes amiss if its shell can be cracked. Cereals, and the seeds of many plants such as the wild buckwheat, buttercup, blackberry and dandelion are much enjoyed. Chippy specially relishes the winged maple seeds which scutter about the garden on a gusty autumn day, and nibbles them with the wing held carefully in her paws. Bulbs and corms find favor on occasion.

Chipmunks drink often, sipping dew from a leaf or water from a shallow pool. In early spring Chippy has been known to break off an icicle hanging from the bird-bath and suck it like a lollipop. Though able to swim, chipmunks prefer to keep dry, but when the water level sinks low in a bird bath Chippy will stop squatting on the rim and climb in to drink more comfortably.

Soft fruit is eaten on the spot because it will not keep, while the seed or kernel is pouched as treasure-trove. Apples, pears, strawberries are all popular, and little heaps of crumpled skins show where Chippy has feasted on deftly peeled grapes. Cherries are favorites, and when they ripen robins, bluejays, catbirds and chipmunks share the harvest chores. In early spring Chippy spends little time near the tree, but as soon as the blossoms fade, she is up in the branches, impatiently nosing among the leaves.

Given sufficient incentive chipmunks climb well, and the hope of a tasty morsel encourages acrobatics. They will somersault on the very tip of a swaying hazelnut twig to nip off a cluster, and shin up a flower stalk for seed. One spring morning Chippy snapped off a tulip head and paused for a moment with it in her mouth, a brilliant scarlet balloon almost as big as herself. Insensitive alike to the beauty of the flower and the charm of her own pose, she briskly stripped the petals to pouch the stamens.

Graciously prepared to experiment, chipmunks brighten their blameless diet with richer fare when circumstances allow. Bread and butter, pastry crumbs, cheese and raisins are welcomed in moderation. After a pause for calculations, very large cookies are cut up for

passage through very small holes. An occasional lick of whipped cream is irresistible, and hardboiled egg a delicacy. It is usually left for a day or two until well covered with interested ants, the chipmunk's caviare. Such gourmet preferences appear to have eluded rigorous analysis by professional zoologists.

A little meat, no doubt, tones up the constitution. In the summer Chippy spends time on the terrace, running her tongue along the cracks to scoop up unwary ants. Mysteriously, she does the same when there are no ants present, licking the paving stones until they are visibly wet. Like squirrels, chipmunks have been known to inspect the insides of car wheels, perhaps in search of squashed insects. The remains of a frog and a salamander have been found in chipmunk stomachs; larvae, snails and slugs in cheek pouches (48). From time to time, Chippy herself develops, and promptly indulges, a craving for worm. Occasionally, chipmunks attack field mice and small birds, whose eggs they also eat, along with fried onions, *rognons sautés* and even *fruits de mer* when available. Gabriel Sagard records that on fishing expeditions with Indian friends he saw ' les suisses ', undeterred by yells and blows, swarming over the catch spread out to dry (49). In short, chipmunks are vegetarians with an open mind on the subject of living protein.

They are not, however, gluttons, being far too concerned with collecting for the future to allow much time for self-indulgence in the present. Because of this, most photographs of chipmunks show them with severe cases of mumps, cheek pouches bulging. These, quite inconspicuous when not in use, are extra-ordinarily capacious. Audubon saw a chip-munk carrying off hickory nuts four at a time: two in one pouch, the third in the other and the fourth between his teeth (50). Six chest-nuts can be squeezed into two pouches, but peanuts, being oblong, fit awkwardly. Only one is popped into each side and a third is held in the mouth like a pirate's cutlass. Often the peanut has to be pushed in and drawn out several times before the most comfortable position is found. Chipmunks remove the sharp points at each end of a nut before stowing it away. Even a full load leaves Chippy free for other activities: drinking, yawning and singing.

When pouches are empty the face is sharp and pointed; when full it is framed with a ruff of fur like a lion's mane. Similarly, a change in position can transform the whole appearance of the body. While hard at work the chipmunk is all muscle, with a slim, elastic frame which will flatten out to squeeze into the narrowest crack. Deep in meditation he becomes a puffball, fur glimmering like gossamer in the sun.

Hard work keeps chipmunks trim. When, on one occasion, Chippy was presented with a giant sunflower head, over one foot in diameter and bristling with ripe seeds, she seemed at first stunned by the splendor of the treasure and the enormity of the task ahead. After a pause she set to work. For the whole of that September afternoon until dusk, and long past her usual bedtime, she toiled to and fro over the distance of several yards between the sunflower and her hole. Only an occasional rest for wash and brush up broke the rhythm of repeated pouchings and journeyings. By the time darkness came, three-quarters of the head had been stripped. At seven the next morning Chippy was already back on the job, and she worked steadily for two more hours before the sunflower head was bare and her larder bursting at the seams. Quite early in

the proceedings she had marked the head with one of her droppings, which proved a most effective deterrent. Another chipmunk, attracted by the excitement, hovered longingly round the seeds during Chippy's frequent absences but never once dared to snatch a prize. The head, signed for and sealed, was Chippy's own.

Mood varies as much as body shape and attitude. Chipmunks can flicker in and out of wall crannies like lizards, or sit up straight and tall, slim as a pencil, motionless but alert to every noise or smell or sudden movement. At other times they sit hunched for long periods like miniature buddhas lost in meditative trance. Often they sing in this position, each 'chip' accompanied by a slight, convulsive jerk. Chippy, when so inclined, will keep this up for minutes at a time, paws folded over velvet stomach, hiccupping discreetly. The quality of the tone varies from a full, fruity 'chip' to a dry little cough, a hacking cough, which gave the chipmunk another of its names, Hacky, popular in the last century and used by Beatrix Potter in *Timmy Tiptoes* for her character Chippy Hacky (51).

The loud, confident song is so familiar a part of the American country scene that Dr. Hollister, searching for Siberian animals early in the present century, almost missed the silent chipmunks there:

> 'The animal is remarkably quiet for a chipmunk and might readily be passed many times unobserved.' (52)

The chipmunk song itself has been interpreted in various ways; as an enigma by the Clackamas Chinook Indians of Oregon:

> 'Only in the fog
> That is when I sit on my haunches.' (53)

and as a natural thermometer by Thoreau:

> 'Some old authority (says) the bark of the striped squirrel is the, or a, first sure sign of decided spring weather.' (*Journal*, March 8, 1853.)

What the song really means is still unsettled. It is not a territorial claim, nor a mating call. Unscientific as it may be, the theory that a chipmunk sings when he is happy seems at this stage as good as any other.

Nothing is unobtrusive about the chipmunk's song or his bold, eye-catching stripes, but it is remarkable what effective camouflage the latter provide in dappled sun and shade. Nabokov in his autobiography describes how a baby almost succeeded in eluding a cat by lying down on its side, when the stripes merged into the pattern of light on the ground (54).

With several natural enemies, the chipmunk's life expectancy when unprotected in the wild is believed to be two or three years. Much to be feared are animals like the weasel and the rat which can squeeze through a tunnel to attack the nest, and many a chipmunk falls victim to a hungry fox, raccoon or snake. In suburban gardens the most formidable adversary is the cat, often found spread out like an old fur rug on the wall, waiting for action. At first sight of it, Chippy freezes to attention, seconds before bolting to safety.

When the large grey squirrel appears Chippy slips away, believing, without claim to originality, that discretion is the better part of valor. There is no hint of crisis, as each acknowledges the facts of life, but with the smaller, fiery red squirrel relations are distinctly strained. Both have peppery tempers, and neither takes kindly to company at mealtimes. Bigger and faster, the red squirrel usually gets his own way, but on one occasion Chippy was so irritated by his poaching that she chased him up and down between bird feeder and wall. After this humiliation, he was not seen for weeks.

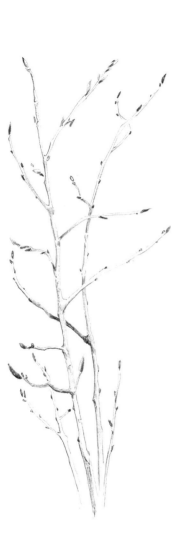

In the normal way, chipmunks tuck themselves in well before twilight, but occasionally linger for a while in the long summer dusk. The owl as well as the daytime hawk can then be a danger. A chipmunk reacts with instant fear to the barred owl's cry, and Audubon painted one dangling from the claws of a barn owl as evening darkens into night (55). Though never yet exposed to any bird enemy, Chippy herself has an intense dislike for the predatory pounce with which bluejays land on the wall. Once they have stopped swooping she pays little further attention, however self-importantly they may strut. In truth, chipmunks themselves are happy enough to pounce when a suitable victim presents himself. While babies were collecting seeds on top of the log pile, a soft, plump rabbit came loping up to a cluster of portulaca flowers at its foot and settled down to munch. As chipmunk babies are inordinately fond of portulacas, one watched with baleful eye, until the rabbit's placid unconcern became intolerable. Chipmunk Jr. sprang through the air and landed on a furry back. Startled out of its wits, the rabbit vanished, and the baby, visibly triumphant, helped himself to the sweetest bud he had ever tasted.

The lightning reactions and speed which are a chipmunk's best defence give him a bold confidence in his dealings with lesser breeds. Chippy speeds for home from the bird feeder through a crowd of birds, not with a furtive scuttle but like a bullet shot from a gun, scattering sparrows as she goes. The stone wall offers ideal ledges for mourning doves, plumped out like bolsters airing in the sun. Chippy will charge past, sometimes cannoning into them. Grackles or bluejays promenading majestically over the rocks are forced to make a little skip as Chippy hurtles on between their toes.

Nowhere is this streak of aggressiveness shown more sharply than in chipmunks' relations with each other. By nature self-contained, they live alone except for the very brief mating period and the weeks when babies are in mother's care. Chippy's range extends to no more than 22 yards from her main entrance, and within this distance are several key points where food is to be found. All are visited regularly by Chippy and two other chipmunks. When they happen to meet there are minor skirmishes, occasionally with a dazzling display of split-second somersaulting, but no major battle. None of the three could be said to ' own ' any of the sites.

The core of Chippy's domain (about 30 square yards) is the rock wall, and there the situation is quite different, leaving no doubt as to who is the poacher and who the enraged

property owner. Chippy charges and the thief
flees. Originally, both parts of the wall, lying
to left and right of the steps, were hers, but in
the summer of 1968 she was toppled from power
by a swift and not entirely bloodless *coup
d'état*.

In June, just as she had finished chasing
away her babies to stake new claims of their
own, a powerful stranger suddenly made his
appearance in the garden. Summer is the
time when young males, born the year before
and now mature, are known to make their

major quests for territory (56). This one arrived in the pink of condition, aggressive, strong and much faster on his feet than Chippy. He was named Genghis Khan, quintessential bully-boy. At first when Chippy attacked he slipped away, but very soon he stood his ground.

Chipmunks become ribbons of fur and muscle when they fight, rolling over and over together, sometimes chestnut backs showing, sometimes white bellies flashing like fishes tumbling in the sea. The aim is to bite, and the favorite places are the tail, the flank and behind the ear. Ferocious as the encounters seemed to be, they were never desperate, judging at least from the fact that Chippy, often attacked while trying to return to the wall with a pouchful of food, never lost her peanut while she wrestled. The moth-eaten appearance of Genghis during the crucial week, with large tufts of fur missing here and there, was visible proof of her ability to bite home even with both pouches bulging.

Nevertheless, Genghis won. The very kernel of Chippy's kingdom was a certain spot on the left wall where she loved to groom herself. When at last the rude intruder was spotted sitting there as bold as brass, washing his whiskers, the end was in sight. First he claimed Chippy's front door. For a day or two she used another, still on the same side, but soon she was forced off the left wall altogether and pushed over to the right. Providently, she had made some tunnels there long before this crisis, and so a new home was ready and waiting for her, but without the food store she had so carefully collected.

For about a week there was the dispiriting spectacle of a rampant Genghis and a furtive Chippy. He patrolled the left wall with swishing tail and eagle eye, ready to shoot off in all directions and in hot pursuit; she crept to safety under cover, skulking behind flower

tubs and scuttling home. Not a trace was left of that exuberant, bouncing run, tail held upright like a banner, which characterizes a chipmunk at ease with the world.

Happily, the situation was capable of improvement and Chippy, gathering her wits, began at last to perceive some age old possibilities. One morning early in July she came out boldly, hopped to the log pile and sat there singing loudly. Genghis darted over to interfere but, instead of retreating, Chippy slowly descended and, still very slowly and deliberately, walked across Genghis' path and disappeared round the side of the house. Just as slowly, he followed her. Much later, in the early evening, they were seen once more, this time both on the right wall, and with roles dramatically reversed. Now it was Chippy who could edge Genghis back onto his own side. Once he had worked his way to the right again they played hide-and-seek, popping in and out between the stones, touched noses and finally vanished into the same hole together. One hour later, both were on the left, both busily washing, a bare yard apart. In a burst of triumph, Chippy shot up the flower bed and flung herself down for an ecstatic dust bath.

There can be little doubt that on this day they mated, though no babies were born afterwards. Chippy continued to live on the right wall and Genghis on the left, but from this time on much of the tension went out of the situation. Each defended his wall and each poached cheerfully on the other's; Chippy grew confident again, and Genghis calm. There is invariably a decline of the male's aggressiveness and power in the late summer and fall (57). As with those sun gods whose strength waxes and wanes from dawn to noon and noon to night, it may be that the power of both sexes ebbs and flows throughout the year. Some observers have found the female to be dangerously fierce towards the male (58). In the spring of 1969 Chippy and Genghis mated again and continued to enjoy a placid co-existence on their respective walls. If anything, Chippy was now the bolder, but no more serious skirmishes were seen. Six babies duly appeared, noted by Genghis without obtrusive fatherly pride but never attacked while on their own ground.

In courtship ceremonies between chipmunks bellicosity is slowly metamorphosed into gentle play. The mating between Chippy and another male in the spring of 1968 took three days to complete. One brilliant, icy morning in early March Chippy was meditating in the sun on the left stone wall. Suddenly she sensed something, turned her head and stiffened in outrage. An intruder was creeping

towards her, flattening himself against the stones. A yard from her he stopped in his tracks. For a moment both were motionless, then Chippy pounced and there was a wild chase to and fro across the flower beds. For the rest of that day and the next Chippy was dominant, the hunter in every chase. She would wash herself with aggressive thoroughness in her favorite place on the wall, while the male crouched gloomily at an acceptable distance. On the second day, while each sat on a separate wall, he was silent but Chippy sang confidently and continuously for minutes at a stretch. The third morning saw a distinct change. Gone were the frozen, heraldic poses, the swift, fierce pursuits, and in their place was a most amiable form of hide-and-seek, in and out of the wall's crannies. Upon any slackening of interest on the male's part, any momentary preoccupation with a peanut, Chippy would peep out and delicately touch his tail or flank to coax him into another little flurry of flirtation. Proof positive of the male's new status was the permission to groom his whiskers in Chippy's special place. In the end he was led up the flower bed to Chippy's front door behind the vine. She shot past the hole, but he waited there until she returned, when the bushy tail and the straight one disappeared together. When next glimpsed, late that afternoon, Chippy was alone. The male had vanished from the garden.

In 1967 the mating took place on the log pile under a window. Again there was much playfulness, and sometimes the two would touch or lick each other's faces very gently near the eyes. However sense, not sensibility, marks the chipmunk character; as the male mounted her, Chippy filched his last sunflower seed. Afterwards they sat peacefully side by side, staring into space.

Considering the chipmunk's preference for independence and solitude, it is remarkable how much time a mother devotes to the upbringing of her family. The period from conception to birth is thirty-one days. In the last week or so Chippy was never out for long, showed little interest in food and spent most of the time collecting soft and rotted leaves for her nest. The outward signs of pregnancy are slight and easily missed by the uninitiated. At the time of birth Chippy did not emerge at all for two days. In the first days after she reappeared she left the nest only for a few minutes at a time, quite indifferent to food but drinking a great deal. As the days wore on she escaped from the nursery to soothing peace for longer and longer periods, staying out sometimes until twilight.

The babies are completely dependent on their mother for several weeks, being born blind, naked, toothless and with ears closed (59). Slowly fur and teeth grow, ears open and the babies begin to move about. At

last, a month after birth, the eyes open and the
family is free to explore its labyrinthine
nursery. At any time from this moment with
a little luck, it is possible, by bending down
beside the wall, to hear soft croonings and
sharp little squeaks, or to look between the
stones and catch a glimpse of small bodies
shuffling in the leaf-strewn tunnel.

Only when six weeks old are the babies ready to climb up into their new world. The day before they appeared in 1968 Chippy was extremely busy. In half an hour she made twenty trips along the wall, transferring rotted leaves from one hole to another. She herself continued to go in and out of her usual front door, but the babies used the newly prepared burrow from the time they emerged to the day they were chased off the property. The customs of one year are not necessarily repeated in another. In 1969 Chippy did not bother to make provision for a separate nursery entrance and had reason to reget the traffic jam at her own front door, while six babies played first-in-first-out. Too late, she set to work, but by the time a new entrance had been completed the babies were gone. From then onward, she used it as her own.

They stay with Chippy about two weeks, a time for exuberant exploration of a garden brimming with late May's abundance. Games of tag, mock fights, playful caresses fill the long, sunny days. Four faces peep out of one hole, one baby pushes another off the wall, two roll over and over like brown leaves among the iris stems. The stones become a himalayan range, conquered by shaky but determined mountaineers. Three babies swarm on a vine tendril while a fourth vainly tries to climb a post much too wide for his leg span. Startled by a sudden noise, one finds himself chimneying

up the inside of a drainpipe, squeaking with alarm, uncertain how to get down again.

Baby gestures are the same as those used in courtship. They climb each other's backs, touch noses, delicately lick round eyes, knead and nibble sides and tails. For several days

they tried to suck Chippy, usually to be crossly pushed away. She would let them take food from her pouches, however, and sometimes touched them softly with her nose. One baby in particular kept very close to her side for a whole week, following her every movement and taking his first trip from wall to log pile under her comforting escort.

After ten days this idyll begins to pall, and Chippy chases the family away. By the end of two weeks even the most determined baby is gone. Chippy can relax at last.

For the chipmunk in his relations with man, familiarity may breed acceptance, but never love. His admirers are left to feast their delusive hopes on tales of mutual devotion like that told by Mrs. Traill in *Stories of the Canadian Forest* (60). Here a man takes his pet chipmunk with him on board a steamboat, where it is stolen from his pocket by an envious peddlar. Providentially, a code has been

worked out before hand between master and pet for just such an emergency. The former only has to whistle the latter's favorite tune for the chipmunk to leap from the peddlar's clutches and make its way unerringly to its friend, singling him out from a crowd of other passengers.

To the less musical chipmunks of today, man is never more than necessary nuisance. As provider of peanuts, he is grudgingly tolerated, especially in public picnic places where man and chipmunk strike a common chord in quest of food. There are reports of chipmunks accepting food from the hand, but Chippy herself has never done this.

For the title of Man's Best Friend, the chipmunk is a poor contender. It is his nature to trust no one. When one is small it is wise to be self-sufficient; when one is small and very charming it is imperative. Wary aloofness is the chipmunk's best defence against man's insatiable desire to cage his favorites. Gulliver hated to be shown off as a plaything by the giant Brobdignagians, but saw nothing amiss in exhibiting the Lilliputians' cattle ' to many Persons of Quality ' when he returned to England. His only regret was that he had been forbidden to carry off any Lilliputians themselves. Chipmunks refuse to dwindle into pets. Their mysterious and complicated lives touch man's here and there, never to become engulfed. Wrapped in the dignity of independence, their trim, determined figures dot his gardens, self-absorbed, self-reliant, self-contained.

NOTES

1. John Lawson, *The History of Carolina* (London, 1718), Preface.
2. *Ibid.*
3. Patrick M'Robert, *A Tour Through the North Provinces of America, 1774-5, ed.* Carl Bridenbaugh (Historical Society of Pennsylvania, 1935), p. 40.
4. Gabriel Sagard, *Le Grand Voyage du Pays des Hurons* (Paris, 1632), *ed.* Emile Chevalier (Paris, 1865). See chapter *Des Animaux terrestres,* section 306.
5. John Josselyn, *An Account of Two Voyages to New England* (London, 1675), reprinted by William Veazie (Boston, 1865), p. 69.
6. Lawson, *op. cit.,* p. 124.
7. Peter Kalm's *Travels in North America (the English version of 1770), ed.* A. B. Benson (New York, 1937), p. 169.
8. Letter of August 1778 from Peter Pallas to Thomas Pennant, in *A Naturalist in Russia, ed.* C. Urness (University of Minnesota Press, 1967), pp. 30-1.
9. Oliver Goldsmith, *A History of the Earth and Animated Nature* (London, 1774), chapter on squirrels.
10. *The Travels of William Bartram, ed.* Francis Harper (Yale University Press, 1958), p. 177.
11. Comte de Buffon, *Histoire Naturelle* (Paris, 1749–67), chapter on squirrels.
12. Thomas Pennant, *History of Quadrupeds,* 3rd edition (London, 1793), Vol. 2, section XXXI, the Dormouse. This begins with the Striped Dormouse.
13. Ernest Walker, *Mammals of the World* (Baltimore, Johns Hopkins Press, 1964), Vol. 2, p. 713f. The notes on the etymology of *tamias* and *eutamias* were kindly supplied by Dr. F. Robertson of the Classics Department, Reading University, England.
14. *The History of a Squirrel Family* first appeared in Catherine Traill's *Lady Mary and her Nurse* (London, 1850), and was reprinted several times in the course of the century in other collections of her stories, for example in *Stories of the Canadian Forest.*

15. Dr. Craig C. Black, in *Bulletin of the Museum of Comparative Zoology, Harvard University* (Cambridge, Mass., December 1963), Vol. 130, no. 3, p. 234.

16. *The Elizabethan's America*, ed. L. B. Wright (Harvard, 1965), p. 187.

17. For the use made of Bartram's journal by Coleridge in his notebook and poems, see J. L. Lowes, *The Road to Xanadu* (Boston, 1930), pp. 8, 46–7, 514.

18. H. Thoreau, *A Week on the Concord and Merrimack Rivers*, in *Works*, ed. H. S. Canby (Cambridge, Mass., 1937), p. 149.

19. Certain similarities in the details of *History of a Squirrel Family* and *Timmy Tiptoes* suggest the possibility that Beatrix Potter may have known Mrs. Traill's story. Miss Margaret Lane, Mr. Leslie Linder and the Curator of Mammals at the London Zoo, Dr. M. R Brambell, were all kind enough to contribute information and ideas towards the solution of this small problem.

20. George Edwards, *A Natural History of Birds* (London, 1743–51), p. 181.

21. Sir Hans Sloane's account quoted in William Jardine, *The Naturalist's Library* (London, no date, mid 19th century?), Vol. 23, *Mammalia*, Introduction, p. 40.

22. Thomas Bewick, *Memoir, ed.* Edmund Blunden (Southern Illinois University Press, 1961), p. 123.

23. *Philosophical Transactions of the Royal Society of London* (1735–6), Vol. 39, p. 389.

24. John Brickell, *The Natural History of North Carolina* (Dublin, 1737), reprinted by the Johnson Publishing Company (Murfreesboro, N. C., 1968), p. 129.

25. *Philosophical Transactions of the Royal Society of London* (1693), Vol. 17, p. 123.

26. For the word chipmunk see articles by A. F. Chamberlain in *American Notes and Queries*, III (1889), and in *Journal of American Folk-Lore*, IX (1896). See also U. S. Bureau of American Ethnology, Bulletin 30, Part I, *Handbook of American Indians*, under *chipmunk*.

27. The material on Navaho chipmunk customs, beliefs and folk tales has been most kindly supplied by Dr. R. W. Lang, Mrs. Nedra Cook and Mr. Harry Walters, all of the Museum of Navaho Ceremonial Art, Santa Fe, New Mexico.

28. S. I. Ognev, *Mammals of the U.S.S.R. and Adjacent Countries* (Jerusalem, 1966), Vol. 4, *Rodents*, p. 398.

29. E. A. Smith, *Myths of the Iroquois* (2nd Annual Report of the Bureau of American Ethnology, Washington, D.C., 1881), p. 80. In a Menomini Indian story, the chipmunk suggested to the other animals that winter and summer should share the year between them, just as the dark and light stripes alternated on his own back. The bear on the other hand, with his plain dark coat, wanted winter to last all through the year. Claude Lévi-Strauss, *L'Origine des Manières de Table* (Librairie Plon, 1968), p. 298.

30. James Teit, *Traditions of the Thompson River Indians of British Columbia* (Boston and New York, 1898), p. 61.

31. This story was communicated by Dr. and Mrs. K. Vedam of State College, Pennsylvania.

32. Charles G. Leland, *The Algonquin Legends of New England* (London, 1884), pp. 146–7. See also Lévi-Strauss, *op. cit.* (in note 29), pp. 193–4.

33. See Harold S. Colton, *Hopi Kachina Dolls* (University of New Mexico Press, Albuquerque, 1949) for an account of kachinas. The chipmunk kachina is no. 56 in his descriptive list.

34. The detail from a Navaho Plumeway sand painting reproduced here was copied by Mrs. Rebecca Lang, of the Museum of Navaho Ceremonial Art, Santa Fe, New Mexico.

35. A. F. Chamberlain in *American Notes and Queries* (1889), Vol. 3, p. 155.

36. *John and William Bartram's America*, ed. Helen Gere Cruickshank (Devin-Adair Co., New York, 1957), p. 310.

37. R. W. Yerger, *The Biology of the Chipmunk in Central New York, with Special Reference to Home Range and Territoriality* (Ph.D. thesis, Cornell University, September 1950), p. 76.

38. Elsa G. Allen, *The Habits and Life History of the Eastern Chipmunk* (New York State Museum Bulletin, no. 314, September 1938), pp. 73–4. See also Yerger, *op. cit.*, pp. 76–7.

39. Josselyn, *op. cit.*, p. 69.

40. Randle Cotgrave, *Dictionarie of the French and English Tongues* (London, 1611), reprinted by the University of South Carolina Press, 1968.

41. This unusually early disappearance in 1968 was followed by an unusually early and heavy 22-inch snowfall on November 12th, whereas the autumn of 1967 was rather mild.

42. For details of chipmunk behavior during hibernation, see Allen, *op. cit.*, pp. 95–108.

43. Allen, *op. cit.*, pp. 19–22.

44. Kalm, *op. cit.*, pp. 170–1. For Russian reference see Ognev, *op. cit.*, p. 415.

45. Allen, *op. cit.*, pp. 75, 81.

46. Ognev, *op. cit.*, p. 415.

47. Pennant, *op. cit.*, p. 157.

48. Yerger, *op. cit.*, pp. 68–9.

49. Sagard, *op. cit.*, chapter 19, *Des ceremonies qu'ils observent à la pesche*, section 260.

50. Allen, *op. cit.*, p. 78.

51. This popular name is recorded for example by John D. Godman in his *American Natural History* (Philadelphia, 1826–8), Vol. 2, p. 142.

52. N. Hollister, *Mammals Collected by the Smithsonian-Harvard Expedition to the Altai Mountains, 1912*, in *Proceedings of the U.S. National Museum* (Washington, 1913), Vol. 45, p. 522.

53. Melville Jacobs, *The Content and Style of an Oral Literature; Clackamas Chinook Myths and Tales* (New York, 1959), p. 201.

54. V. Nabokov, *Speak Memory* (G. P. Putnam's Sons, New York, 1966), p. 224.

55. Allen, *op. cit.*, p. 93. J. J. Audubon, *The Birds of America*, ed. W. Vogt (New York, 1965), plate 171.

56. Yerger, *op. cit.*, p. 26.

57. *Ibid*, p. 51.
58. Allen, *op. cit.*, p. 57.
59. For the slow development of babies from birth see Allen, *op. cit.*, pp. 43–57.
60. Catherine Traill, *Stories of the Canadian Forest* (Boston, no date, circa 1860), chapter 6, pp. 108–9.

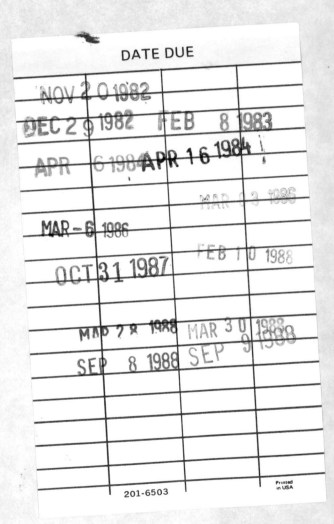

DATE DUE

NOV 2 0 1982		
DEC 2 9 1982	FEB 8 1983	
APR 6 1984	APR 1 6 1984	
		MAR 3 1986
MAR - 6 1986		
OCT 31 1987	FEB 1 0 1988	
MAR 2 8 1988	MAR 3 0 1988	
SEP 8 1988	SEP 9 1988	
201-6503		Printed in USA